SHED BASHING IN THE 1970S AND 1980S

Colin Alexander

Front cover (upper)
A nocturnal scene at Nottingham's Toton shed, *c.* 1984, with a pair of Class 56s along with new No. 58007. (Ian Beattie)

Front cover (lower)
One of Gateshead's shunters, No. 03079 stands with her match wagon on the 'ash-heaps' on 8 March 1983. (David Tweddle)

Rear cover
At Kingmoor, north of Carlisle in April 1983, No. 40033 carries a painted version of her long-removed *Empress of England* nameplates. (David Tweddle)

First published 2018

Amberley Publishing
The Hill, Stroud
Gloucestershire, GL5 4EP

www.amberley-books.com

ISBN 978 1 4456 7646 3 (print)
ISBN 978 1 4456 7647 0 (ebook)

British Library Cataloguing in Publication Data.
A catalogue record for this book is available from the British Library.

Origination by Amberley Publishing.
Printed in the UK.

Introduction

1970 heralded the dawning of Britain's first decade without steam (with the exception of *Flying Scotsman* and other preserved locomotives) on the main line.

Many enthusiasts abandoned British Railways when steam ended in 1968, either hanging up their cameras or joining the nascent preservation movement. Others continued with their hobby on BR's totally dieselised and electrified network, and a new generation took up their Ian Allan ABC books on Britain's steam-free railway.

Even by 1970 many non-standard or unsuccessful diesel types, some less than ten years old, were extinct, but there was still plenty of traction variety if you knew where to look.

At that time there were almost forty different classes of diesel locomotive and ten types of electric loco in use on BR, plus countless variants of diesel and electric multiple units. Although corporate 'monastral' blue livery was introduced in the 1960s, many locomotives were still in their old colour schemes of green, maroon or even 1950s black.

The TOPS renumbering programme changed the identity of locomotives that survived the standardisation cull, and by the end of the 1980s, the number of diesel locomotive types was reduced to about a dozen. The same TOPS system saw the arrival of a new shed-code system too, so for example Gateshead changed from the 52A to GD.

By the time my dad was taking me, aged six or seven, to watch the trains, the writing was on the wall for several types. I clearly remember seeing Clayton Type 1s, also known as Class 17s, on freight around Tyneside, and a long line of them dumped at the back of Tyne Yard. During a family stay in London about 1971 I have dim memories of a visit with Dad to Paddington station, whose roof reverberated to the distinctive sound of the Maybach engines of diesel-hydraulics. The highlight though was the sight of one of the doomed Blue Pullman sets in the later, duller livery and with multiple-working cables disfiguring its sleek lines.

Dad introduced me to many lineside vantage points, such as Yanwath, near Penrith; Lamesley, south of Gateshead; and Sessay, north of York. My favourite, though, was the classic location on top of the Norman castle keep overlooking the diamond crossing at the east end of Newcastle Central. Among my most precious possessions are some of Dad's colour slides taken from here in the early 1970s.

In September 1972 I got my first taste and smell of an engine shed, for Thornaby depot near Middlesbrough hosted an open day, with ex-LNER A4 No. 4498 *Sir Nigel Gresley* as the star attraction.

As I grew up in the mid-1970s, my railway activities were mostly limited to preserved railways, with the notable exception of family holidays in Cornwall in 1973 and 1976, during which Western diesel-hydraulics featured heavily.

It wasn't until 1978, at the age of fourteen, that I was allowed to go independently to Newcastle Central station. The total cost of a child fare return from Tynemouth along with a platform ticket was less than 10p. I quickly made friends with other lads on Platforms 9 and 10 at the Central, forming lifelong friendships. Forty years later, we still go on railtours and to preserved diesel galas together.

The west end of Newcastle Central gave us a tantalising glimpse across the Tyne of locomotives stabled at Gateshead depot. It was only a matter of time before the temptation became too great. A short walk past the castle and along the lower deck of Robert Stephenson's High Level Bridge brought us to the entrance to the old North Eastern Railway Greenesfield Works and on into Gateshead sheds. Making the mistake of politely knocking on the foreman's office door, we were quickly chased off. Next time we knew better and just sneaked in. The best way to do this was to scramble up the bank at the west end of the shed beside the King Edward VII Bridge to gain access through a gaping hole in the fence to the sidings known as the 'ash heaps'. Although we were out of sight of the office in those pre-CCTV days, we did once have a close escape when we'd just gotten back down the bank as the British Transport Police arrived.

The BTP were kept busy by us 'spotters'. While a coach-load of Durham enthusiasts stood on the edge of the golf course overlooking Sheffield's Tinsley shed, one of the youngest of the group was sent into the shed yard to scribble down the numbers. He was spotted by a female BTP officer, and in a scene straight from *The Benny Hill Show* she chased him as he weaved nimbly between the locos. Skilfully avoiding her, he managed to get each and every number.

We soon progressed to travelling, usually with the excellent £2.60 weekly Northumbrian Ranger ticket. We mostly 'bashed' Deltics between Berwick and York but always made time to visit Carlisle, and the border city's Kingmoor shed. This was one of our classic days out, by train along the Tyne Valley for a bus from Carlisle city centre to the Redfern pub, and then down the road to Kingmoor shed. On all but one occasion we were flatly refused entry by the 'gadgie' in the office, so we'd trudge back gloomily over the bridge again, forced to view the locos on the shed across the main line from the weed-infested rusty sidings opposite, where once stood the great steam shed. These sidings would often contain a bonus in the shape of withdrawn locomotives awaiting disposal, and following the sidings to their north end brought us to one of our favourite vantage points, the old 'Waverley route' bridge, and a view of the secondary shed in the huge marshalling yard.

It is difficult to imagine in today's era of health and safety and accountability that enthusiasts were ever allowed to access such facilities, but back then most depot staff were at least tolerant, and at best welcoming.

Once we began to travel further afield in our quest for more exotic locomotives, we found the Scottish Region foremen at Edinburgh's Haymarket, Inverness and Glasgow's Eastfield and Polmadie sheds were far more amenable to scruffy youths wandering about their territory than their Gateshead and Kingmoor counterparts.

The Ian Allan *Locoshed* series of books became an indispensable part of our armoury, providing directions to traction depots and lists of locomotive allocations. In those far-off days before Google Maps, the trusty *Locoshed Directory* was unerringly accurate in guiding legions of scruffy teenage lads through drab suburban Britain to the depot gates from obscure railway stations and bus stops. That book did not, however, guarantee our safety, for these sheds were frequently located off the mean streets of some of the dodgiest parts of Britain's towns and cities.

On an eventful first-time-ever trip to Liverpool in 1979, we got 'arrested' by the BTP for the heinous crime of going the wrong way on a moving escalator in Lime Street station. Having been reprimanded we were freed and allowed to proceed with our plan of 'doing' both sheds in Birkenhead.

Having used the Merseyrail system under the river to get to the Wirral, I somehow lost my ticket and had no cash, and therefore had no means of boarding a train back to Liverpool. Imagine the look on the ticket vendor's face when I asked where the nearest bridge was, thinking I could simply walk back over the river. I now know that it is approximately a 25-mile walk to the bridge at Runcorn. Fortunately he took pity and let me fare-dodge back under the Mersey.

Whole weekends would be planned around shed bashes. Just after my sixteenth birthday six of us travelled overnight from Newcastle to London. Three of us travelled in style behind Deltic No. 55012 *Crepello* to York, and then No. 55009 *Alycidon* the rest of the way to the capital, arriving in the early hours of Saturday morning. The other three lads were not so well off, so they met us at Victoria, having caught the overnight National Express coach. This rendezvous in the capital was somehow managed despite the absence of mobile phones.

With the *Locoshed Directory* and my Dad's 1950s A-Z in my pocket, we visited Clapham Junction and then the Southern Region sheds at Selhurst and Hither Green with their Class 73 electro-diesels. Then followed the Eastern Region trainspotters' mecca of Stratford, complete with some of the last remaining Pilot Scheme Class 31/0s. The North London line took us to Willesden Junction, where the Midland Region's AC electrics awaited us, and then it was down the road to the Western Region's Old Oak Common to see Class 50s and named 47s. Our trip was concluded with more Deltic haulage behind No. 55014 *The Duke Of Wellington's Regiment* overnight from King's Cross, with diversions via Lincoln and the Leamside line, while our mates suffered another night on the M1 and A1. We all got home early the next morning, tired and filthy but very happy.

A couple of the Durham lads were almost bursting with excitement as they travelled from Derby station to the massive Toton depot in 1979. They asked the bus driver to let them know when they got there. He forgot and they ended up in Nottingham city centre. The driver did get them there on his return and the boys set out on a mad mission to 'cab' every engine on Toton shed. Some considerable time later, two exhausted gibbon-like creatures staggered away with lolloping limbs, weary from hauling themselves up dozens of pairs of handrails to cab doors. As they passed the signal box their misplaced sense of achievement evaporated as one exclaimed 'What about 08xxx at the very back of the shed! We've bloody missed one!!!' So back they trudged to tick off their hundredth 'cab' of the day!

At some sheds it was simply impossible to obtain permission for a look around, with one such being Holbeck in Leeds, but in those instances it was usually possible to find a viewpoint over a bridge parapet or by climbing a fence. Some locations were best viewed from a passing train, which at speed meant that a photographic memory for multiple numbers became handy.

In contrast to the hostility experienced at Holbeck and Gateshead, one correspondent remembers the friendly Welsh shed foreman at Margam phoning his colleagues at Swansen's Landore and Cardiff's Canton sheds to tell them to expect him and his mate within a couple of hours!

As if the varied contents of BR's engine sheds were not interesting enough, it was even more exciting to visit the various workshops of British Railways Engineering Ltd (BREL), which were normally accessible only on open days. Dad came up trumps in June 1978 and September 1979, taking me to Doncaster and Crewe open days. These events introduced me to the unforgettable smell of the paint shops and the fascinating sight of disassembled locomotives undergoing overhaul.

Visits to BREL's works also offered the opportunity to see new locomotives under construction, as well as the sad sight of others at the end of their lives awaiting disposal by oxyacetylene torch. A friend remembers being at a Derby open day, being part of an army of children trying to dismantle 138 tons of withdrawn 'Peak' for souvenirs.

The most memorable open day for me was the incredible 'Deltic D-Day' at Doncaster, on 27 February 1982. Thousands of enthusiasts converged on the town to pay their last respects to the last survivors of the class, all having been withdrawn from service and seven having already been cut up. Hearts raced with a mixture of excitement and sadness as some of the lads stepped off the OK Motor Services bus from Durham outside the works gates, to hear one of the slumbering beasts burst into life!

Open days were fine and enjoyable, but their very legitimacy meant they weren't a patch on blagging our way into a depot or works where we shouldn't have been! We would negotiate the hazards of rusty barbed wire, brambles and nettles in order to achieve our goal. The unofficial way into Doncaster Works involved a long walk around its perimeter along 'Dog**** Alley', and through a hole in the fence that was perilously close to the murky River Don, into which one of my mates almost tumbled.

There was an impromptu 'open day' at Inverness shed when Deltic No. 55009 *Alycidon* took a 'Merrymaker' excursion from Newcastle to Perth to be replaced by a pair of Class 27s to the Highland capital. On arrival at Inverness everyone piled off the train, jumped off the platform and straight across the track under full view of the signal box and into the shed! The foreman was the last to know. No. 40167 took the trespassers on to Aberdeen for No. 55009 to take them back to Tyneside.

Angry depot foremen and barbed wire weren't the only dangers associated with bunking engine sheds. My friend Tim and I, then aged twelve and fourteen respectively, had been taken by his parents to Glasgow for the day. The grown-ups set off shopping, leaving us kids to have fun visiting Eastfield shed. Like many BR depots it was surrounded by run-down estates and industrial dereliction, and we soon became aware we were being followed. Turning around, I saw a boy about our age, but looking much 'harder' than us (not difficult). He was accompanied by a much older lad who looked even scarier. What really caught our eye though was that one was wielding a half-brick while the other carried a bike chain. We ran as fast as we could but Tim's legs could not carry him as fast as mine did me. I made it to the security gates of the Metal Box factory and got the guards there to rescue Tim. Our assailants scarpered but not before robbing Tim of what little cash he was carrying.

The police were called and we soon found ourselves in a scene from *Rab C. Nesbitt*, riding the mean, tenemented streets in a 'jam sandwich' squad car on the lookout for the baddies. Our description of the older of the two matched that of one of their most wanted, a lad they had been after for a while, and soon enough we spotted him. He and his young sidekick were hauled into the back seat and the former was literally sat on by the arresting officer for the journey to the 'nick' – six of us jammed into a five-seater car!

Their pockets were emptied, the contents given to us, and we were sent on our way. A tidy profit was made and nothing was said to my friend's parents.

Another Eastfield trip was like a surreal scene from Golding's *Lord of the Flies*. This one took place during a Rail Enthusiasts' Society All-Scotland Shed Bash in April 1980. The coach driver took a wrong turn very close to Eastfield, ending up in a cul-de-sac between the tower blocks. In the Wild West, when under attack by the natives, the cowboys formed a circle of wagons, but that's not easy with one vehicle. The Glaswegian natives rained missiles on the coach from above and, astonishingly, among the silhouetted youths was an assailant in a nappy, throwing stones from one of the blocks of flats!

Some of the other perils associated with shed visits were inspection pits, oily puddles, tripping hazards and moving trains. Southern Region depots and Birkenhead offered a 750 V DC third rail as an additional danger, but we are all still here. I cannot recall a single tale of any young enthusiast meeting with an accident while bunking a shed, so either we were all endowed with good old-fashioned common sense, or we were just lucky.

Unlike the numerous Class 47, more than 500 of which could be found almost anywhere on the BR network, or the even more ubiquitous Class 08 shunter, some locomotive types were associated with a particular region, route, or even depot. Mention, for example, Toton shed to any enthusiast of a certain age and they will think of the ten Class 44 'Peaks' that were shedded there for many years.

The trans-Pennine Woodhead route was another such location, with its 1,500 V DC overhead supply. South Yorkshire's subsidised bus fares at that time cost us kids 2p per journey. That princely sum would get us from Sheffield or Doncaster to the exotic weekend destination of Wath, where several of the venerable Class 76 electrics could be admired. Their home depot of Reddish in Manchester presented the unique sight of locomotive bodies removed from their bogies and dumped on the ground. I kept a bulb from one of No. 76002 headlamps in a sweetie tin for years.

Another trainspotters' 'holy grail' in those long-gone days was Holyhead breakwater on Anglesey. Isolated from the main network, this outpost shed housed BR's two remaining Class 01 diesel shunters, which were very camera shy. They retained their original 1950s black livery long after the rest of the diesel fleet had been repainted, first green, and then blue.

On one occasion, a Llandudno-bound 'Merrymaker' excursion had carried a couple of the Durham lads as far as Llandudno Junction where they changed trains for Holyhead. Having trudged the long walk to the breakwater they climbed through a gap in the boarded-up shed window to 'cop' the 01s. Next time they vowed to return with a camera. Tickets were bought for the next trip and they decided to take their bikes this time. One slight problem was that one of the bikes had just been sold to another school pal. Negotiations were concluded and a loan arrangement was put in place for the weekend.

On the train, all was going well as the Class 40 slowed for Llandudno Junction station, but the guard was nowhere to be seen as the double doors of the guard's van were pulled open in readiness to alight with the bikes. By now down to a slow crawl, the train drew alongside the platforms, still decelerating, and the front wheel of the first bike was poked out of the doors. Suddenly, all hell broke loose as the turbocharged whistling sound of the Class 40 erupted, signifying that stopping at the 'Junction' was not on the schedule of this year's 'Merrymaker'. A quick-thinking grab of the collar on the part of his mate saved both him and his friend's new purchase! After that near-death experience, a service train took our heroes to Holyhead, where a quick cycle ride to the breakwater and the same snake-hips manoeuvre got them into the shed. Kodak 126 film did not always produce the best results, and having eagerly awaited the film's return from the chemist some disappointment was expressed that this thrilling adventure had resulted in yet another frame of 'Instamatic' well and truly wasted.

Another mate remembers a Rail Enthusiast bus tour to Glasgow Works open day. En route, the driver stopped at Berwick-upon-Tweed at about 3 a.m. in order to 'cop' the Class 03 shunter there. Not everyone was best pleased at being woken up at such an unsocial hour, just for a Gateshead-based diesel shunter!

Meanwhile, our intrepid Holyhead cyclist had organised a minibus from Durham to the same Glasgow event. Its driver almost killed everyone at Gateshead, being unaware of the incomplete flyover that had been intended as an approach road to an aborted Tyne crossing. Before crash barriers and planters took up residence on the truncated end of it there was a wide strip of road in the centre with a fence and a drop immediately beyond it. It was a tight swerve, but the minibus just made it down the slip road!

In this book I have assembled a collection of photographs that show a wide variety of traction in the principal depots and works all over the network, along with many of the lesser installations. They are arranged principally in the order of BR depot codes.

Special thanks to my old friend David Tweddle, whose photographic collection was the inspiration for this book. Also thanks to Ian Beattie, Craig Oliphant, Paul James, Lewis Bevan, Mike Mather, Trevor Casey and all of the other photographers for their valuable contributions. Thanks are also due to the excellent BR Database website.

Shed Name	Location	Pre-1973 Code	Post-1973 Code
Aberdeen Ferryhill		61B	AB
Ashford Chart Leacon		73F	AF
Allerton	Liverpool	8J	AN
Ayr		67C	AY
Birkenhead Mollington St		8H	BC
Botanic Gardens	Hull	50C	BG
Barrow Hill	Staveley	41E	BH
Brighton		75A	BI
Cambois	North Blyth	52F	BL
Bury		9M	BQ
Bristol Bath Road		82A	BR
Bescot	Walsall	2F	BS
Buxton		9L	BX
St Blazey	Par	84B	BZ
Cambridge		31A	CA
Crewe Diesel		5A	CD
Cardiff Canton		86A	CF

Shed Name	Location	Pre-1973 Code	Post-1973 Code
Chester		6A	CH
Cockshute	Stoke-on-Trent	-	-
Colchester		30E	CR
Coalville		17C	CV
Cricklewood	North London	14A	CW
Dundee		62B	DE
Doncaster		36A	DR
Dunfermline Townhill		62C	DT
Eastfield	Glasgow	65A	ED
Edge Hill	Liverpool	8A	EG
Eastleigh		70D	EH
Ebbw Junction	Newport	86B	EJ
Exeter St Davids		83C	EX
Frodingham	Scunthorpe	36C	FH
Finsbury Park	North London	34G	FP
Gateshead		52A	GD
Gloucester Horton Road		85B	GL
Grangemouth		65F	GM
Glasgow Shields Road		-	GW
Haymarket	Edinburgh	64B	HA
Holyhead		6J	HD
Hither Green	South London	73C	HG
Healey Mills	Wakefield	55C	HM
Holbeck	Leeds	55A	HO
Immingham	Grimsby	40B	IM
Inverness		60A	IS
Kingmoor	Carlisle	12A	KD
Knottingley		55G	KY
Laira	Plymouth	84A	LA
Landore	Swansea	87A	LE
Llandudno Junction		6G	LJ
Longsight	Manchester	9A	LO
Leicester		15A	LR
Margam	Port Talbot	87B	MG
Millerhill	Edinburgh	64A	MH
Motherwell		66B	ML
March		31B	MR
Newton Abbot		83A	NA
Newton Heath	Manchester	9D	NH

Shed Name	Location	Pre-1973 Code	Post-1973 Code
Neville Hill	Leeds	55H	NL
Norwich		32A	NR
Northwich		8E	NW
Old Oak Common	West London	81A	OC
Peterborough		-	PB
Perth		63A	PH
Polmadie	Glasgow	66A	PO
Reading		81D	RG
Reddish	Manchester	9C	RS
Ryde	Isle of Wight	70H	RY
Shirebrook	Mansfield	41J	SB
Sunderland		52G	-
Stratford	East London	30A	SF
Stewarts Lane	South London	75D	SL
Springs Branch	Wigan	8F	SP
Severn Tunnel Junction		86E	ST
Selhurst	South London	75C	SU
Saltley	Birmingham	2E	SY
Thornaby	Stockton-on-Tees	51L	TE
Tinsley	Sheffield	41A	TI
Thornton Junction	Fife	62A	TJ
Toton	Nottingham	16A	TO
Tyne Yard	Gateshead	-	TY
Upperby	Carlisle	12A	-
Wath	Wath-on-Dearne	41C	WH
Willesden	West London	1A	WN
Worcester		85A	WS
Westhouses	Alfreton	16G	WT
Westbury		82D	WY
York		55B	YK
BREL Crewe		-	ZC
BREL Derby		-	ZD
BREL Doncaster		-	ZF
BREL Eastleigh		-	ZG
BREL Glasgow		-	ZH
BREL Swindon		-	ZL

An everyday 1970s view of Aberdeen Ferryhill sees Birmingham Railway Carriage & Wagon Co. (BRC&W) Class 26 No. 26021 stabled with two classmates and a Class 27 on 9 April 1977. No. 26021 was introduced in 1959 as D5321 and was withdrawn in 1991. At the time of the photograph she was allocated to Inverness. (The late Steve Chambers, courtesy of Kier Hardy)

A uniquely Southern Region scene at Ashford Chart Leacon. Parked outside the heavy repair sheds during an open day on 14 August 1982 are Nos 024 and 001, former electric multiple units in Departmental use. No. 024 was converted in 1973 as an engineers' stores unit. Note the wooden shuttering providing some protection to personnel from the live third rail. (Adrian Nicholls)

Allerton depot outside Liverpool was host to English Electric Class 83 No. 83008 on 29 February 1976. She was allocated to Longsight in Manchester, and was built at Vulcan Foundry in 1960 as E3031. The 83s were formerly Class AL3, being one of five types ordered for the first stage of the West Coast Main Line electrification. No. 83008 was withdrawn in 1983. (Lewis Bevan)

There were diesel sheds off the BR network too. The NCB in Northumberland had a fleet of ex-BR Class 14 diesel-hydraulics, mainly at Ashington. The depot staff there were extremely tolerant of enthusiasts, and in February 1983 the former D9504 is seen with two sisters. Two years earlier I had enjoyed a cab ride in her at nearby Weetslade. She was built at BREL Swindon in 1964 and was withdrawn from BR service in 1968. Remarkably, she was later employed in the construction of the Channel Tunnel rail link and is now preserved at the Kent & East Sussex Railway. (David Tweddle)

Ayr shed was host to BRC&W Class 27 No. 27039 on 1 August 1974. The 26s and 27s were at this time almost exclusive to Scottish lines, making occasional ventures south to Carlisle or Newcastle. Built in 1962 as D5398 and originally allocated to Cricklewood, No. 27039 was an early casualty, being withdrawn in 1975. (Trevor Casey)

No. 25100 was built at BREL Derby in 1964 as D5250 and is seen here at Birkenhead Mollington Street on 15 July 1979. No. 25100 was an example of the redesigned Class 25 with tidier bodysides and no end communication doors. She was withdrawn in 1981. It was on a visit to this depot that I discovered there was no easy way back across the Mersey to Liverpool without money in the pocket! (The late Steve Chambers, courtesy of Kier Hardy)

Hull's main depot was Botanic Gardens. Among the locomotives stabled here on 21 October 1984 were No. 08248, No. 37006 and No. 31451. No. 37006 was built by English Electric in 1961 as D6706, later becoming No. 37798, in which guise she was eventually withdrawn in 2005. No. 31451 was built by Brush of Loughborough as D5852 in 1962 and was renumbered 31318. She became No. 31451 when fitted with electric train heating only a month before the photograph was taken, and she was withdrawn in 1996 as No. 31551. (Lewis Bevan)

We can still experience that engine shed atmosphere at Barrow Hill, for it survives as a preservation centre. Inside the roundhouse on 21 March 1981 are almost-new Nos 56077 and 56090 (in 'large-logo' livery), standing by the turntable in the company of No. 08509. On this day my mates and I were travelling from Newcastle to Plymouth and back via Edinburgh, London and Southampton, on a trip that involved fourteen separate train journeys. They included haulage by three different Deltics and seven Class 50s! (Andy Hoare)

The roundhouse forms a distant backdrop to this view of the yard at Barrow Hill on 28 July 1984. Several locos of Classes 20, 37 and 56 can be seen, all resting from hauling coal trains around the Derbyshire and Nottinghamshire area. The disc-headcode-fitted Class 20 in the centre of the photograph is No. 20046, built as D8046 at Vulcan Foundry in 1959 and withdrawn in 1993. (Lewis Bevan)

Viewed from the lofty vantage point of Terminus Road on 7 June 1977, Brighton shed is host to six of the Southern Region's Class 73 electro-diesels. The first of these emerged from Vulcan Foundry in 1962 and some are still in service today. A twelve-car SR EMU passes on the main line and another rests at the depot along with a departmental unit. (Rex Holt)

From the south coast to the shores of the North Sea. Situated a few hundred yards from the sand dunes was Cambois, close to the site of the former North Blyth steam shed. It provided traction for coal trains supplying the nearby power station with Northumbrian coal. This early 1980s view shows five members of Class 37. They would be replaced by the new Class 56s before coal traffic ceased and the depot closed. (Ian Robinson)

Bury depot housed a unique fleet of DC EMUs for the Manchester service. In the early 1970s the redundant steam shed adjacent was used to store a number of electric locomotives. On 10 April 1971 they included Class AL4 (later 84) E3037, later No. 84002, and Woodhead route prototype Class EM1 No. 26000 *Tommy*, built in 1941. E3037 would be refurbished at Doncaster, ultimately becoming No. 84002 and lasting in service until 1980, but *Tommy* was already withdrawn and was destined for scrapping at Crewe. (Gordon Edgar)

Bristol Bath Road was one of those rare depots that could be viewed from a station, or as in this case, from a passing train. Taken from the 09.30 ex-Paddington hauled by Class 52 1028 *Western Hussar*, No. 45048 *The Royal Marines* and No. 50031 are centre stage with a cast of Class 31s, 47s and other 50s in the background on the date of the American bicentennial, 4 July 1976. (Arnie Furniss)

So much of Bath Road could be seen from the platforms of Temple Meads station that it is unusual to see photographs taken within the confines of the depot. One such shot shows No. 46032 on 1 October 1983. Built in 1962 at Derby and allocated to Gateshead for much of her life, she was a stalwart of the north-east to south-west route, and lasted until 1984. (Paul Lyons)

Apart from the Class 08 shunter, the Brush Class 47 was the most numerous diesel type on BR. Until the late 1970s, of the 512 built, only seventeen of the Western Region examples were graced by a name. One of these, No. 47076 *City of Truro*, is seen at Bath Road in June 1983, with the distinctive clock behind. She was built in 1965 as D1660, and she is still in service today with Colas Rail as No. 47749. (David Tweddle)

On the same gloomy day in June 1983, English Electric Class 50 No. 50029 *Renown* is viewed from Temple Meads station on the approach to Bath Road shed. Built at Vulcan Foundry as D429 in 1968 and withdrawn in 1992, she is preserved at Peak Rail in Derbyshire. (David Tweddle)

Bescot depot was in a large marshalling yard near Walsall. A wide variety of traction could be observed here on inter-regional freight traffic. Illuminated by the winter sunshine of 30 January 1983, No. 40174 was parked outside the shed there. Built in 1962 at Vulcan Foundry as D374, she was withdrawn in 1984. (Dave Jolly)

Bescot on 6 October 1984 saw No. 56075 with a classmate, along with a Class 45 and a 47. With the main depot north-west of the station often being difficult to access, it was considerably easier to take photographs on the opposite side of the line, as seen here. No. 56075 was built at Doncaster in 1980 and withdrawn in 2004. (Phil Richards)

The small depot at Buxton in Derbyshire was home to the DMUs needed for the town's passenger service. It also acted as a stabling point for freight locomotives, such as Nos 47369 and 45020 captured there on 15 July 1984. No. 47369 was one of the freight-dedicated subclass, built at Brush in 1965 as D1888 and scrapped by 1998. No. 45020 was a product of Derby Works, entering service in 1961 as D26 and lasting until 1985. (John Crooks)

St Blazey was just outside Par in Cornwall and boasted a distinctive half-roundhouse arranged around its turntable. Mainly used to stable locomotives used on china clay traffic, on 22 September 1985 it housed Nos 37247, 50017 *Royal Oak* and 37222. The 1874-dated building is a unique survivor from the steam age and as such is a listed building. (Ron Westwater)

Cambridge was principally a DMU depot but on 27 November 1982 this small, utilitarian building housed No. 40024 and some departmental rarities. Class 24 ADB968008 was formerly No. 24054, and ex-Class 31/0s ADB Nos 968015 and 968013 (previously Nos 31014 and 31013 respectively) were employed here for a short time as carriage-heating units, bringing complaints of noise from nearby residents. No. 24054 is now preserved at the East Lancashire Railway. (Craig Oliphant)

As befitted such an important railway town, Crewe Diesel was a major depot. In this 1975 view the shed hosted two formerly named Class 40s: No. 40012 *Aureol* and No. 40027 *Parthia*. No. 24141 is also visible along with another Class 24. *Aureol* is still with us, beautifully preserved in working order, and recently took part along in the Class 40s' 60th birthday gala at the East Lancashire Railway. (David Hopkins)

The term Traction Maintenance Depot (TMD) was attached to many of the larger BR depots, and, as the name suggests, they had the facilities for repairs and examinations. Crewe Diesel was one such shed and in 1987, close to the end of her working life, No. 25176 can be seen jacked up from her bogies. (Ian Charles)

In the early 1970s, diesel-hydraulics from the Western Region were regular visitors to Crewe, adding to the wide variety of traction that could be enjoyed there. In June 1970, Class 52 D1061 *Western Envoy* rests in the company of a Class 40 and a 47. (Mike Mather)

Also in June 1970, English Electric Class 50 D423 is seen on shed at Crewe. At this time, the West Coast Main Line was electrified from Euston to Crewe, Manchester and Liverpool. The Class 50s were employed north of here over Shap and Beattock to Glasgow, often double-headed. Apart from the Class 55 Deltics they were the only BR diesels permitted to run at 100 mph. (Mike Mather)

Enthusiasts with local knowledge of Cardiff Canton approached the office via the Leckwith Road entrance, seeing everything 'around the back' first. For those who had been thrown out of the depot with veiled threats of prosecution, the footbridge was a handy vantage point, as seen on 3 August 1974. Forty years later it was gone, and the Westerns and Peaks, one of each of which is in the foreground, are a distant memory. Several 37s and 47s survive in use on the main line today though, possibly including some of those seen here. (Arnie Furniss)

The Class 52 diesel-hydraulics were the first BR diesel class to gain a sizeable cult following among enthusiasts. 1976 was their last full year in service and on 3 July of that year No. 1036 *Western Emperor* stands outside the shed at Cardiff Canton alongside a filthy Class 37. The handsome profile of the Westerns was designed to match BR's Mk 1 coaching stock. (Stephen Burdett)

By 3 May 1980 the walls of Canton depot no longer reverberated to the sound of the Western Maybach engines. Viewed from the footbridge, Gateshead's No. 46029 awaits her next turn, probably on the north-east to south-west route on which the Class 45s and 46s were a staple for many years. A departmental-liveried Mk 1 brake second is stranded, rail-less, in the background. (Trevor Casey)

When BR's 'large logo' livery appeared in the late 1970s, it certainly brightened up the railway landscape, marking a departure from more than a decade of the dull corporate blue scheme. On 23 August 1988, Nos 47547 and 47537, the latter with her large bilingual *Sir Gwynedd/County of Gwynedd* nameplates, stand next to Canton's footbridge. No. 56034 and an unidentified Class 31 are wearing the Railfreight grey version of the livery. (Greg Brookes)

By the time I was an independently travelling railway enthusiast, the 151-strong Class 24s had been reduced to three survivors in traffic. In previous years they were a familiar sight around the north-west. No. 5045 was photographed at Chester depot in the early 1970s. She was withdrawn in August 1975 as No. 24045. (Trevor Casey)

The line-up at Stoke-on-Trent's Cockshute stabling point on 22 January 1978 includes Class 47, 40, 08 and 25 diesel-electrics. Inside the shed is a Class 104 DMU and electric multiple units of Classes 304 and 310 stand beyond that. Despite its size, Cockshute did not have a two-letter TOPS code. (Mike Henney)

Colchester shed on 2 May 1971 was host to a trio of diesel shunters. D2284 was a Drewry Class 04 built at Robert Stephenson & Hawthorn in Darlington. She was withdrawn a few weeks before this photo was taken but saw further use with the NCB in Yorkshire. She is now preserved by the Heritage Shunters Trust at Peak Rail. Her BR-built equivalent, Class 03 No. 2051, was withdrawn the following year and worked for Ford at Dagenham before preservation at the North Norfolk Railway. Meanwhile, Class 08 No. 3692, tucked inside the shed, is still in service with Freightliner, numbered 08530. (Gordon Edgar)

A variety of diesel classes could always be found at Coalville, close to the M1, especially at weekends. One of the freight-only Class 47/3s with no train-heating boiler, No. 47347 is stabled with Railfreight-liveried No. 58023 on 30 August 1985. Behind is celebrity green Class No. 40122/D200, now part of the National Collection. (Mark Bugler)

Cricklewood shed was the London depot for the Midland line out of St Pancras. In the 1980s the main locomotive type used on Sheffield trains was Class 45/1. No. 45149 shares the modern shed with Class 317 electric multiple units for the Bedford service. The Peak was withdrawn by the time this photograph was taken on 7 April 1988, but is preserved at the Gloucester & Warwickshire Railway. (Michael J. Collins)

Contrasting with the modern functionality of Cricklewood is the steam-age architecture of Dundee shed. This atmospheric view, taken on 25 January 1981, shows three Metro-Cammell DMUs of Class 101 and a single diesel railcar of Class 122. The inspection pits can be seen, one of the many hazards negotiated by shed bashers. (Bruce Galloway)

Doncaster shed was always worth a visit, and its staff were usually happy to let us wander, despite its proximity to the main line. Gleaming ex-works locomotives, fresh from the nearby works, could often be seen, such as this unidentified Class 31/1 on 31 July 1982. (Colin Alexander)

Dunfermline Townhill was a Scottish Region depot used for stabling freight locomotives. Weekend visits to such depots yielded many locomotives and Saturday 23 July 1983 rewarded the photographer with the sight of English Electric No. 20117 lined up with Nos 26014, 26013, 20013, 20040 and 20108. (Neil Young)

Staying in Scotland and following on from No. 20117 we have No. 20118 at Eastfield, Glasgow, in August 1982. This was another shed where spotters were given a free rein to wander. The Class 20 is accompanied by No. 27103, one of the Class 27/1s formerly used in pairs on the Edinburgh–Glasgow 'push-pull' services until replaced by Class 47/7s. (David Tweddle)

That same dreich August day saw one of Eastfield's long-term residents, No. 27043, looking rather worse for wear. She had been withdrawn from traffic in 1980, and was used for re-railing exercises, replacing No. 24006, which was in a similar state when I had visited in 1979. No. 27043 was finally put out of her misery in 1985 at the hands of the scrap man. (David Tweddle)

No. 37081 was one of Eastfield's favourites, being named *Loch Long*, and was used on the West Highland line. Note the Highland terrier logo below her nameplate. She was captured on film at her home depot in August 1982. Eventually renumbered No. 37797, she was finally withdrawn in 2003 after forty years of service. (David Tweddle)

Ten years earlier, in September 1972, Class 24 5001 looks resplendent beside Class 27 5351. The 24 had been withdrawn and reinstated in 1969, and would last in service until 1975 by which time she was renumbered No. 24001. She was the second BR Sulzer Type 2 to be built, following D5000 in 1958. No. 5351, meanwhile, became No. 27005 and survived until 1987. (Mike Mather)

Edge Hill was a stabling point outside Liverpool Lime Street. With a gantry for overhead electric wires forming a backdrop, Sulzer-engined pair Nos 25172 and 46055 wait for their next turns on Sunday 16 October 1977. In the case of the Class 46, it is likely to be a Newcastle service. (Douglas Johnson)

Eastleigh depot in Hampshire was one of the Southern Region's biggest facilities. Among the SR's unique classes were the fourteen-strong Ruston & Hornsby Class 07 shunters, employed mostly at Southampton docks. Two members of that class, Nos 07001 and 07010, are stabled with No. 33031 on 9 August 1977. Both of the '07s' are preserved. (Rex Holt)

Also at Eastleigh that day was No. 74008, one of the ten Class 74s rebuilt at Crewe in the late 1960s from Class 71s. They were more powerful than the English Electric Class 73 electro-diesels and were used on boat trains to Weymouth. They shared the same Paxman diesel engine as the Western Region's Class 14 diesel-hydraulics. All were withdrawn by the end of 1977. (Rex Holt)

This Eastleigh scene taken on 11 March 1984 is pure Southern Region. From left to right we have an ex-Southern Railway utility van, BRC&W Class 33/1 No. 33113, '4-SUB' unit No. 4733 from a batch introduced in 1949, and later '2-HAP' unit No. 6166. The 33/1s were fitted for push-pull working and could be driven from the front cab of a '4-TC' set while propelling it. (Gordon Edgar)

Probably one of the last photographs taken of the unique Brush prototype Class 53 No. 1200 *Falcon,* at Ebbw Junction, Newport, on 20 March 1976. The former D0280 had been withdrawn a few months earlier, in October 1975, and just a few days after this photograph was taken she was towed the short distance to Cashmore's scrapyard, where she was quickly cut up. Just visible on the extreme right is the photographer's 1966 Wolseley. (Lewis Bevan)

With Exeter St Davids station providing an excellent viewpoint, Exeter depot was one of the most photographed. By 21 November 1987, a Southern Region influence is evident with BRC&W Class 33s Nos 33050, 33021 and 33055 joined by shunter No. 08941. Also present is modified Class 50 No. 50149 Defiance, re-geared for freight work as a one-off experiment. She is now preserved in her previous guise of No. 50049. (Adrian Nicholls)

Still wearing her 1960s green livery, Brush Type 2 No. 5637 rests between duties at Frodingham, Scunthorpe, on 27 April 1973. She would soon be renumbered 31213, and then much later 31465. Still surviving in 2018 at the age of fifty-eight, she is now owned by Harry Needle Railways Ltd and is based at the Weardale Railway. (Trevor Casey)

Finsbury Park in north London received its allocation of 3,300 hp English Electric Napier Deltics from 1961. The eight of them were named after racehorses, in the LNER tradition. In 1979 and 1980 the cult status of the depot's six survivors was enhanced when they were adorned with white cab surrounds, as seen on No. 55009 *Alycidon* in May 1981. She is preserved in working order by the Deltic Preservation Society. No. 31220 stands alongside. (Paul James)

The sidings of Gateshead's 'ash-heaps' were at the opposite end of the shed to the foreman's office and were accessible to Tyneside's intrepid enthusiasts. At least one Class 03 diesel shunter could usually be found there, and on 8 March 1983 here is No. 03079 complete with her match wagon, attached to ensure track circuit operation. Happily she is preserved at the Derwent Valley Railway. (David Tweddle)

The running lines that link the King Edward and High Level bridges, and connect the main line from Durham to the coast line, passed to the south of Gateshead shed. Here in February 1983, No. 37013 leaves the fuelling point and heads west, possibly for Tyne Yard. In the background part of the old Greenesfield Works can be seen. (David Tweddle)

A twenty-first-century visitor to this spot would barely be able to tell there had once been a major engine shed here. The tower blocks in the background survive, much refurbished, but of Gateshead shed there is little trace. On 8 March 1983, Class 08 shunters Nos 08373 and 08274 stand beside No. 46044. All three of these locomotives would be withdrawn by 1985. (David Tweddle)

While Finsbury Park and Haymarket each had eight Deltics, Gateshead was allocated the remaining six, and all were named after regiments based in the North Eastern Region. No. 55017 *The Durham Light Infantry* was instantly recognisable due to the unique size of her nameplates, and although seen here at her spiritual home in 1981, she was, like her sisters, by this time allocated to York. (Ian Robinson)

By February 1983 Gateshead's Deltics were but a memory, so its flagship locomotives were now its 'generator' Class 47s. No. 47402 *Gateshead* is in the filthy condition that was so typical of locos allocated to her namesake depot. She is now beautifully restored to original condition in two-tone green livery as D1501 at the East Lancashire Railway. (David Tweddle)

Not something I personally ever saw, this view shows the interior of the usually impregnable Gateshead shed. The depot had an allocation of Class 46s for many years, seeing use mostly on services to the south-west. No. 46030 appears to be receiving some attention as she stands over one of the inspection pits on 14 April 1974. (Trevor Casey)

Visually similar to the Class 46s were the 45s, differing mainly in the type of traction motors installed. The Class 45/1 variant were those fitted with electric train heating, and one of these, No. 45139, is seen at Gloucester Horton Road on 4 March 1983. (The late Steve Chambers, courtesy of Kier Hardy)

Two Class 37s and a 27 stand idle at Grangemouth shed in Scotland in 1982. Situated in the industrial heartland of Scotland, this depot served the local heavy freight traffic. The young enthusiast in the shorts will be in his mid-forties now and the person taking his photograph, whom I assume to be his father, appears to be wearing a high-visibility vest. (Ian Robinson)

Glasgow Shields Road was home to BR's Class 81 electric locomotives as well as the iconic 'Blue Train' electric multiple units, later Classes 303 and 311. One of the latter is in the background of this shot, showing a much shorter-lived occupant – one of the ill-fated APT-P Advanced Passenger Trains, No. 370006, seen in August 1980. Her nose section is lifted to permit shunting. (Craig Oliphant)

Haymarket in Edinburgh on 5 July 1971 is the location for another short-lived type seen in Scotland. Clayton Class 17s D8588 and D8603 have Class 40 D367 between them, along with Class 27 No. 5415. I have vague memories of these unreliable centre-cab Type 1s around Tyneside in the late 1960s. All 117 were withdrawn by the end of 1971, and some had gone as early as 1968, being in service less than four years! Miraculously, one, D8568, survives in preservation at the Chinnor & Princes Risborough Railway. (Dave Jolly)

Among the locomotives present at Haymarket on this day in September 1982 was No. 20202. Originally numbered D8302, she was one of the batch of 100 English Electric Class 20s ordered by BR to replace the aforementioned Class 17s. Beyond it is No. 20080, one of the earlier series, and No. 20137. Any disadvantages the EE Class 20s had in terms of crew visibility were vastly offset by their superb reliability record. (David Tweddle)

The Class 20s were one of the success stories of the BR Pilot Scheme, as were the Class 26s. One of the original twenty locomotives ordered from BRC&W for that programme was D5314, later No. 26014. She was captured on film at Haymarket in August 1982, and is preserved on the Caledonian Railway at Brechin. (David Tweddle)

No. 26037 was one of the second order of Class 26s and she can be seen in this September 1982 Haymarket view behind No. 47702 *Saint Cuthbert*. The latter was converted in 1979 from No. 47504 for push-pull working the Edinburgh–Glasgow service, for which the extra jumper cables can be clearly seen. (David Tweddle)

Haymarket's eight Deltics were named after Scottish regiments, and two of them are seen at their 'home' shed in August 1980. By this time they had been concentrated on York shed, but ask any Deltic man and he will tell you that Nos 55019 *Royal Highland Fusilier* and 55022 *Royal Scots Grey* are Haymarket locos. Both survive in preservation. (Craig Oliphant)

Separate from the main BR network, the little shed at Holyhead breakwater held two real gems. Still in their original black livery and carrying the long extinct 'lion and wheel' emblem, Barclay Class 01s Nos 01001 and 01002 were the sole occupants. The photographer recalls that on 12 September 1979 the staff were really co-operative, moving equipment and maximising lighting. He suspects it may have had something to do with the presence of his lovely wife! (Bill Atkinson)

Hither Green in south-east London was on our itinerary when my mates and I did our first shed bashing trip to the capital. A few months before our visit, No. 33062 stands outside the depot on 14 July 1979, with another 33/0 hidden inside. The ninety-eight members of this BRC&W-built class were a bespoke design for the Southern Region. (The late Steve Chambers, courtesy of Kier Hardy)

Another Southern Region speciality was its fleet of third-rail electric locomotives. Twenty-four Class 71s were introduced from 1958 for prestigious continental services like the Golden Arrow and Night Ferry. By 1 June 1978, the glory days for No. 71004 were over, having been withdrawn in November 1977, and she languished at Hither Green, awaiting her final journey to Doncaster for scrapping. (Lewis Bevan)

On 8 September 1983 this line-up at Healey Mills near Wakefield consisted of condemned Nos 40187, 08172, 40148, 40094, 40087 and 40025. Concealed beyond the furthest Class 40 are two departmental rarities in the shape of ADB Nos 968009 and 968001, formerly No. 24142 and D8233. The latter survives in preservation as the only remaining Class 15, and is being restored at the East Lancashire Railway. (John Crooks)

Holbeck was usually viewed from passing trains leaving Leeds, and occasionally by shinning up a handy lamp post. This once-great steam shed was reduced to a roofless fuelling point but a variety of locomotives could usually be seen here, as on New Year's Day 1981 when members of Classes 31, 47, 45, 40 and 08 were at rest. (Les Hyde)

A steam-age relic in the shape of the coaling stage dominates this nostalgic shot of No. 37252 and an unidentified Class 47 at Immingham, near Grimsby, on 25 February 1979. The huge dock complex here, established by the Great Central Railway, generated high volumes of freight traffic. (The late Steve Chambers, courtesy of Kier Hardy)

An even more impressive structure at Immingham was the LNER-built coaling tower, which survived until February 2018. The only example still standing in Britain now is that at Carnforth in Lancashire. Dwarfed by the once-prominent landmark on 11 May 1985 are, from right to left, Nos 37069, 47299, 47295, 47105, 47358 and 47222 *Appleby Frodingham*. (Gordon Edgar)

One of the original twenty Pilot Scheme BRC&W Type 2s, No. 26014 is tucked away inside the shed at Inverness on 8 April 1977. As D5314 she was delivered new to Hornsey depot in North London in 1959, moving a year later to Scotland where she lasted in service until 1992. (The late Steve Chambers, courtesy of Kier Hardy)

The exterior of Inverness shed featured these boldly striped doors, outside which No. 27203 is stabled on 27 March 1982. Sister loco No. 27102 is on the extreme left. Both of these locomotives had been converted for push-pull working on the intensive Edinburgh–Glasgow shuttles, but had by this time been replaced by Class 47/7s. (Colin Alexander)

The photographer has entered the hallowed ground inside Kingmoor shed in September 1982 to get a shot of a Class 40 over the illuminated inspection pit and between the jacks. Most TMDs were equipped with such equipment, capable of lifting the heaviest locomotives from their bogies to allow maintenance on traction motors, brakes and wheelsets. (David Tweddle)

One of the less numerous first-generation DMU types was the Class 100, built by the Gloucester Railway Carriage & Wagon Co. Forty two-car sets were built and this is one of the first batch, by now in departmental use at Kingmoor in 1981. Withdrawals had begun in 1972. Three vehicles of this type survive in preservation. (Colin Alexander)

BR Sulzer Class 25 No. 25080 and a Class 40 enjoy the September sunshine in 1982 outside Kingmoor depot. No. 25080 shows the earlier style of Class 25 superstructure, with several bodyside grilles and the smaller centre windscreen to accommodate the old end communication doors. (David Tweddle)

The English Electric Class 40 was closely associated with Kingmoor and here are three celebrated examples. Nearest the camera are two of the twenty-five locos that were named after ocean liners, although by the time of this April 1983 photograph their nameplates had long since been replaced by painted versions. No. 40033 was *Empress of England* and beyond her is No. 40027 *Parthia*. Third from the camera is No. 40122, formerly D200 and first of the class. (David Tweddle)

By October 1982 there were very few diesel locomotives displaying anything other than simple marker lights in their former train-description panels. No. 40162 was one such example, displaying the meaningless '0000'. She is parked up outside Kingmoor with another DMU rarity, a Class 103 Park Royal unit. Only twenty of these were built, for the London Midland Region, and like the Class 100 seen above, three vehicles are preserved. (David Tweddle)

Also with her headcode panel intact in 1982, Class 81 electric locomotive No. 81007 is captured at the buffer-stops outside Kingmoor. 100 locomotives of Classes AL1–AL5 (later 81–85) were ordered for the LMR electrification scheme out of Euston. Collectively these locos were known as 'Roarers' by enthusiasts, and one of each type is preserved, four of which are at Barrow Hill. (Colin Alexander)

Knottingley depot was a regular calling point on many spotters' itineraries, being easily accessible by public transport and having a perfect vantage point, as seen here. Ferrybridge Power Station forms the dramatic background to this typical 1988 South Yorkshire scene, with wall-to-wall Class 56s displaying four different liveries at this transitional time. They include Nos 56054 and 56110. (Martin Corbett)

Laira depot, on the eastern edge of Plymouth, was one of the Western Region's purpose-built diesel maintenance depots, dating from the early 1960s. 1041 *Western Prince* is in the company of two classmates in one of the gloomier recesses of the shed on 9 August 1974. Happily, she is one of seven preserved, and resides at the East Lancashire Railway. (Trevor Casey)

My only visit to Laira was on an open day, on 25 April 1982. For the record, I got No. 46009 from Newcastle to Bristol, then No. 50022 *Anson* onward to Plymouth. An HST shuttle was provided from North Road station to Laira shed. My return journey was *Anson* again to Gloucester for No. 45102 to take me to Birmingham and then No. 86230 to Stockport. A Class 100 DMU took me to Stalybridge and then No. 47523 took me home to Newcastle! Meanwhile, at the open day here are Nos 50023 *Howe* and 50019 *Ramillies*. (Colin Alexander)

This pleasing shot shows off not only the distinctive architecture of Laira shed but also the classic lines of the 'Western' diesel-hydraulic. No. 1069 *Western Vanguard* was captured on film on 12 August 1973, the year of my first summer holiday in Cornwall and one which featured my first time being hauled behind one of these Maybach-engined beasts. (Trevor Casey)

Two more Western Region diesel-hydraulic types are seen at Laira on 31 August 1971. On the left is one of the unsuccessful North British Class 22s, but taking pride of place is No. 821 *Greyhound*, a Swindon-built Class 42 Warship. Based on the successful German V200 class, they had a superb power-to-weight ratio but their non-standard nature was their undoing on a diesel-electric-dominated British Rail. No. 821 is one of two preserved. (Trevor Casey)

I must confess that at the time they were introduced, my friends and I ignored the InterCity 125 High Speed Train fleet because they had replaced our beloved Deltics. They are still in frontline service after more than forty years, so even I must admit they have been a total success. 3 February 1982 sees a line-up of four Western Region HSTs awaiting their next duty, having been serviced at Laira depot. (Mark Bugler)

Landore depot, just outside Swansea was notable for its Class 03 shunters with reduced-height cabs for working the restricted Burry Port & Gwendraeth Valley line. No. 03382 is seen there in January 1983, obviously awaiting attention for she is missing her coupling rods and has her leading axle supported by a wheel-skate. (David Tweddle)

Like Laira, Landore boasted a modern diesel shed, which can be seen in this view of No. 37180, also in January 1983. By this time BR was allowing more locomotives to carry names, and this example was bilingual, being in Welsh and English: *Sir Dyfed/County of Dyfed.* Two of Landore's Class 08 shunters, Nos 08658 and 08664, complete the scene. (David Tweddle)

The 309 members of Class 37 were reliable workhorses wherever they were allocated, and some are still operational on the network today. Nowhere were they worked harder than in South Wales, and here we see No. 37287 undergoing maintenance inside Landore shed in January 1983. (David Tweddle)

Llandudno Junction was a well-known location to bashers on the North Wales coast line, and was a well-known haunt of Class 40s in their final years. Inside the old shed building on 12 February 1983 is No. 40060. She was one of seven Scottish Region '40s' whose original disc headcodes and end communication doors were replaced by four-character train description panels. (David Peacock)

Variety on show inside Llandudno Junction in this shot taken on 7 May 1983, with No. 25228 most prominent. She was built at BR's Darlington Works in 1963 as D7578 and was withdrawn ten months after the date of this photograph. She is joined here by Nos 25140 (note the different designs of bodyside), 08023, 40091 and 40129. (Andrew Salmon)

The attractive two-tone green livery applied to the later style of Class 25 lingered on many members of the class well into the 1970s. No. 7554, later No. 25204, is outside Longsight shed in Manchester with another in corporate blue and a third '25' of the earlier design in plain green with a pale grey stripe. The date is 23 September 1973. (Trevor Casey)

Probably the most glamorous of BR's diesel-mechanical multiple units were the Class 124 'Trans-Pennine' sets, with their wraparound windscreens. Introduced for inter-city services on the route between Hull and Liverpool, they originally included buffet cars. At Longsight on 17 June 1979 a four-car set led by E51951 rests between duties. (The late Steve Chambers, courtesy of Kier Hardy)

Another city centre depot with a convenient overlooking viewpoint was Leicester, just north of the station. Nos 20077, 56085 and 56116 are among its residents on 24 February 1985. Anyone visiting this location in 2018 is likely to find Class 56s there now. (Lewis Bevan)

Stabled among the oil drums of Margam near Port Talbot on 16 September 1979 are Nos 56037, 45048 *The Royal Marines*, 45077 and 56041. The depot opened in March 1964 and maintained locomotives for South Wales' extensive heavy freight traffic, including that from the nearby steelworks. (Gordon Edgar)

Millerhill depot was situated by the marshalling yard of the same name, just south of Edinburgh alongside the former 'Waverley route' to Carlisle. The line-up on 23 August 1986 includes Nos 20203, 20223, 20219, 20218, 20205 and a solitary Class 47, with Nos 37023, 37056 and 08421 in the background. (Mark Jobling)

The former steam shed at Motherwell is the location for this portrait of No. 20013, taken *c*. 1982. Introduced as part of BR's Pilot Scheme, D8013 was one of the original batch of twenty English Electric Type 1s, and she was in service from 1957 to 1991. A Class 37 and a 25 can be discerned in the gloom of the shed. (Ian Robinson)

Moving from industrial Lanarkshire to the fens of East Anglia, March was an important junction served by a major locomotive depot. Nearby Whitemoor marshalling yard was once the largest in Britain. No. 40152 is seen at March shed, framed by the locomotive washing plant on 20 November 1982. (David Simmonds)

A wide variety of diesel types could be found at March, but by 11 June 1988 it was being used to store withdrawn locomotives, such as No. 45133, formerly numbered D40. She had been taken out of service just over a year earlier, but happily she is preserved at the Midland Railway Centre at Butterley. (Trevor Casey)

Diesel-hydraulics D1021 *Western Cavalier,* D1048 *Western Lady* and D1015 *Western Champion* at Newton Abbot *c.* 1976, together with a Class 45 diesel-electric. While D1021 met the cutter's torch at her Swindon birthplace in 1979, the other two Westerns are still with us, at the Midland Railway Centre and the Severn Valley Railway respectively. (Chris Hallett)

In the early 1980s Newton Heath depot on the northern edge of Manchester plays host to No. 40058, two Class 45s and a BRC&W Class 104 DMU. The '40' appears to be undergoing maintenance, having several access hatches open. Situated next to the Rochdale line, the depot is still in use today for Pacer and Sprinter units. (Ian Beattie)

Normally housing little more than HSTs, DMUs and shunters, Neville Hill depot, east of Leeds, would be low on most spotters' agenda. A touch of glamour was present for an open day on 22 April 1979 in the shape of Deltic No. 55006 *The Fife & Forfar Yeomanry* alongside HST No. 254009 and a Mk 1 sleeping car. Note the young lad leaning out of the coach window! (Lewis Bevan)

Outside Norwich shed on 11 June 1988, No. 47116 shows off the trademark silver roof worn by Stratford's '47s'. As D1704 she was one of five Brush Type 4s originally equipped with a Sulzer V12 power unit, and known as Class 48. In this condition she was once allocated to Norwich shed. All were subsequently re-engined with the standard twelve-cylinder version. (Trevor Casey)

Inside Norwich shed, Class 104 driving trailer E56187 stands beside departmental train-heating unit ADB968015, formerly No. 31014, on 28 September 1981. Entering service in 1958 as D5514, she spent her working life allocated to Stratford, apart from a short spell at Ipswich. Along with her 262 sisters, her unreliable Mirrlees power unit was replaced by an English Electric engine – in her case in 1968. (Paul James)

A pair of Class 25s stand outside Northwich shed in Cheshire, on 9 October 1971. No. 5212 and first of the class No. 5151 became Nos 25062 and 25001 respectively. Detail differences can be seen, for example the fairings below the bodyside on No. 5151, which were present only on the first twenty-five members of the class. These were designated Class 25/0 and were visually similar to the later members of Class 24. (Dave Jolly)

Thirteen years have elapsed at Northwich and all of the Class 25/0s have been withdrawn. Members of Classes 20 and 47 rest inside the main building as No. 40143 stands outside, on 6 July 1984. Only twenty of the 200 examples of Class 40 had the split headcode boxes, the previous 125 being built with disc headcodes, and the last fifty-five having a central four-character display. (David Hird)

Old Oak Common was the main Western Region shed for the capital, located beside the main line out of Paddington. One of the handsome Beyer-Peacock Hymek diesel-hydraulics, No. 7022 stands outside on 27 August 1972. Note the cast numbers, unique among BR diesel classes, and on which the 'D' prefix has been painted out, being redundant since the end of steam. (Trevor Casey)

One of the beneficiaries of BR's relaxed naming policy, No. 47500 *Great Western* received her nameplates in 1979 and is seen beside the turntable at Old Oak Common in December 1982. This Class 47 would find further fame when in 1984 she was selected, along with Nos 47079, 47484, 47628 and 50007, for repainting into Great Western Railway style green livery to mark the 150th anniversary of that famous company. (David Tweddle)

Two products of Brush's Falcon Works in Loughborough are seen side-by-side at Old Oak Common shed in August 1982. Like No. 47500 above, No. 47513 was named in 1979, and carried her *Severn* nameplates until withdrawal in 1997. An unidentified Brush Type 2/Class 31 stands alongside. (David Tweddle)

An entire class that was named in the late 1970s was the English Electric Class 50. All fifty of them were named after Royal Navy warships, many of them duplicating names previously used on the Western Region's diesel-hydraulics. Lurking in a gloomy corner of Old Oak Common depot on a dismal day in December 1982 is No. 50006 *Neptune*. (David Tweddle)

A classic Old Oak Common turntable view is captured here in July 1982, where ten years earlier diesel-hydraulics would have stood. Diesel-electrics rule the roost as Nos 50016 *Barham*, 50030 *Repulse*, 50033 *Glorious* and 47547 provide a comparison between the standard BR blue livery and the then-new 'large-logo' variation. (David Tweddle)

Again at Old Oak Common in December 1982, No. 50028 *Tiger* looks the business, having been recently refurbished at Doncaster. In my opinion this livery suited most locomotives to which it was applied, and especially the Class 50s, which, at 68 feet 6 inches, were lengthy machines. The large numerals certainly aided many a myopic trainspotter! (David Tweddle)

A number of diesel types could be seen at Peterborough shed, but it was fairly unusual to find a Deltic there. Finsbury Park's No. 55018 *Ballymoss* was a visitor on 3 November 1979. The plume of smoke tells us that she is starting one of her twin Napier engines. (Lewis Bevan)

Tantalising glimpses of the stabling point at Perth could be obtained through the arched openings in the station wall. This intrepid photographer has gone to the other side and captured No. 26026 with a classmate and a Class 27 on 6 April 1983. (David Hopkins)

Polmadie was a major depot situated south of Glasgow beside the main line to Carlisle. Snowplough-fitted No. 24121 was resident on 10 April 1977, by which time she was withdrawn from service. As D5121 she had been delivered new to Inverness shed in 1960 and this photograph shows the steel patches over the twin sealed-beam headlights that had been fitted for the Highland line. (The late Steve Chambers, courtesy of Kier Hardy)

Andrew Barclay of Kilmarnock built thirty-five of these 204 hp shunters for BR, and those that survived long enough became TOPS Class 06. They were used exclusively in Scotland. No. 06008, formerly D2437, was withdrawn in 1980 after twenty years of service and is seen here *c.* 1982 at Polmadie, awaiting scrapping. (Ian Robinson)

As well as the thirty-eight Class 42 Warships built at Swindon, North British in Glasgow constructed a further thirty-three locomotives to the same basic design but powered by MAN engines built under licence. Designated Class 43 they were less reliable and had shorter lives. Recognisable by the ventilation holes below her headcode panel, a Class 43 stands at Reading shed in July 1970. (Mike Mather)

Another unsuccessful North British type on the Western Region was the Class 22 diesel-hydraulic, an example of which, D6336, is also at Reading in July 1970. She was one of the last of her type to be withdrawn, on New Year's Day 1972. All fifty-eight were scrapped but a power unit survives and there are tentative plans to build a replica locomotive around it. (Mike Mather)

Giving far better value for taxpayers' money was the BRC&W Class 33. They were frequent visitors to Reading. Class 33/1 D6580 was the first of the class to be fitted for push-pull working, having been converted in 1966 and is seen here in July 1970. She became No. 33119 under TOPS renumbering and was withdrawn in 1989. (Mike Mather)

The long-lived Class EM1, later Class 76, electric locomotives were based at Reddish, on the outskirts of Manchester. On 5 March 1983, almost two years after the Woodhead route was closed and the class withdrawn, No. 76032 and three of her sisters await the end in their purpose-built shed. She met the cutter's torch the following month in Sheffield. A Swindon-built Class 120 DMU is on the left. (The late Steve Chambers, courtesy of Kier Hardy)

Also at Reddish, a week later on 12 March 1983, a BRC&W Class 104 DMU and one of the 1,500 V DC EMUs of Class 506 built for the Manchester–Glossop–Hadfield service share part of the shed with a Class 45 diesel locomotive. The inspection pits in the 'four-foot', together with the clutter of a maintenance depot, present an obstacle course to the unwary. (Paul Lyons)

The only BR diesel locomotive on the Isle of Wight was also the last-surviving example of a Hunslet diesel shunter on the network. No. 2554 was one of sixty-nine such 0-6-0s built by the Leeds firm for BR, and is seen at Ryde on 5 August 1972. Later renumbered 05001 and 97804, she is now preserved at the Isle of Wight Steam Railway. (Dave Jolly)

Shirebrook, near Mansfield, was one of those unglamorous depots that provided motive power for heavy freight traffic. By 11 May 1985, much of this was in the hands of BR's Class 56, exemplified here by Nos 56119 and 56127, in the company of No. 08783. The two 56s here were barely two years old, and both would last into the twenty-first century. (Gordon Edgar)

The first twenty Brush Type 2s, or Class 31s/0 as they became, were part of BR's Pilot Scheme. They spent much of their humble lives at Stratford in East London, where No. 31002, the former D5502, was pictured in March 1979. By this time, the Mirrlees engines installed in them and their 243 more powerful derivatives had been replaced by more reliable English Electric units. (Grahame Wareham)

Stratford's Class 31/0s were withdrawn by 1980 but a few had their working lives extended in departmental use as carriage-heating units. ADB968016 had been No. 31008 and is seen at her old home depot with No. 25177 in December 1982, where they both awaited scrapping. First of the class D5500 is preserved in the National Railway Museum wearing her TOPS identity of No. 31018. (David Tweddle)

A Class 37 line-up at Stratford in December 1982 featuring six members of the 309 that were built. No. 37053 is nearest the camera, followed by Nos 37105, 37115, 37070, 37001 and 37094. The class was used on everything from heavy unfitted freight to express passenger over most of the BR network, with the exception of the Southern Region. (David Tweddle)

Stratford in December 1982 is also the location of No. 40025, carrying her former name *Lusitania* in painted form. Sadly, she had been silenced forever, having been withdrawn two months earlier. She would be scrapped at Doncaster in 1985. Encountering withdrawn and stored locomotives during a shed bash was always poignant, especially when we had previously seen the machines in action. (David Tweddle)

Another part of the fascinating selection at Stratford in December 1982 comprises a Cravens Class 105 DMU along with departmental locomotives ADB Nos 968001 and 968009. As we have already seen, by 1983 these two relics found their way to Healey Mills. They were previously British-Thomson-Houston Class 15 D8233 and BR Class 24 No. 24142. (David Tweddle)

Stewarts Lane depot is tucked away among the railway viaducts and warehouses of Battersea. In the diesel era it was very much associated with the Class 73s, all forty-nine of the versatile electro-diesels being allocated here. On 17 September 1988, No. 73108 stands outside the modern building in InterCity livery. The 73s are another enduring product of English Electric's Vulcan Foundry and many are still with us today. (Trevor Casey)

Springs Branch, Wigan, was another major depot that was visible from passing trains, but it was always more satisfying to visit on foot. I managed one visit here, in August 1979. A month earlier, one of its own allocation of Class 40s, No. 40091, is in the company of No. 25196 and another '25' outside the depot on 15 July 1979. (The late Steve Chambers, courtesy of Kier Hardy)

Shortly after withdrawal and removal from Kingmoor, No. 25044 stands outside Springs Branch in October 1985. Formerly D5194, the locomotive was built at BREL Derby in 1963 and first allocated to Toton. She was eventually scrapped at Doncaster. (Chris Arnold)

One of the batch of '40s' built at Robert Stephenson & Hawthorn in Darlington, No. 40120 of Longsight depot is undergoing maintenance between the lifting jacks inside Springs Branch on 8 March 1980. Beginning life as D320, she gave twenty years of service to BR, from 1961 to 1981. A classmate is stabled alongside. (Ian Charles)

It was unusual to shed bash nocturnally, but my mate did just that at Wigan circa 1982. No. 40169 is captured with some '25s' outside the depot. Withdrawal came for the former D369 in 1983. She spent the first half of her twenty-two-year working life allocated to various London Midland Region sheds but by the 1980s she was a Healey Mills locomotive. (Ian Beattie)

I only ever saw the depot at Severn Tunnel Junction from speeding trains as we passed. Judging by the evidence of this shot taken on 20 April 1987, it would have been worth a proper visit, for there are at least thirty locomotives visible here, comprising mainly Class 37s and 47s. Part of the extensive marshalling yard can be seen beyond. Its location was on the north bank of the Severn estuary, between Newport and Chepstow. (Mick Page)

I visited Selhurst shed, in south-east London, in March 1980 armed with my Kodak Instamatic camera. Needless to say there was not one photograph worth sharing. Eight years later, on 20 March 1988, this photographer was properly equipped and captured this gem inside the depot. Departmental vehicle RDB975010 was known as *Test Coach Iris*. She started life as M79900, a Derby lightweight railcar, as part of BR's first generation of diesel passenger units. She is preserved on the Ecclesbourne Valley Railway. (Adrian Nicholls)

Saltley was one of the most frustrating locations, being one that I passed countless times on the north-east approach to Birmingham, but I only ever glimpsed a small fraction of what was 'on shed'. No. 56027 is surrounded by Class 58s on 15 June 1986. The first thirty Class 56s were imported from Electroputere in Romania, with 105 following from BREL Doncaster and Crewe. (Roddy MacPhee)

Sunderland's old shed kept its steam-era smoke ventilators well into the diesel age, as can be seen above with Nos 37038, 37006 and 37072 as they rest inside between freight duties on 8 December 1984. Formerly known as 52G, the depot never received a two-letter TOPS code. English Electric's Type 3 or Class 37 was another of BR's diesel success stories, and many are still in service in 2018, having been introduced in 1960. (Douglas Johnson)

Thornaby, serving Tees Yard near Middlesbrough, was one of the biggest sheds in northern England. English Electric Type 3 No. 6731 is seen at her home depot on a snowy 30 October 1972. A month earlier my Dad had brought me here, aged eight, on what was my first ever depot visit, to a memorable open day featuring preserved LNER A4 Pacific No. 4498 *Sir Nigel Gresley* in steam. No. 6731 became No. 37031 and was in service from 1961 to 1994. (Trevor Casey)

Thornaby was principally for freight locomotives, so it was unusual to find passenger stock there. These examples of Mk 1 and Mk 2 coaches were presumably there for tyre turning when seen, on 18 November 1984. Nos 31119 and 40135 parked alongside are both preserved, at the Embsay & Bolton Abbey Steam Railway and the East Lancashire Railway respectively. (Robert Patterson)

Standing over an inspection pit inside Thornaby shed in about 1982 is one of the ubiquitous Brush Class 47s, which could be seen almost everywhere on the BR network. Two of the North East's stalwart Class 37s are on the other road. Thornaby was notable for its 1957 roundhouse, the last built for steam on BR. (Ian Robinson)

One of the BR depots that was famous for having its own unique class was Tinsley, to the north of Sheffield. The huge marshalling yard there required something more powerful than the standard Class 08 shunter, so in 1965 six of them were selected for conversion to three permanently coupled 'master-and-slave' units, in which one of the cabs was removed from each pair and extra weight was added. No. 13001 is seen inside the maintenance shed on 25 March 1984. (David Chamberlain)

In the summer of 1988, the last of BR's Class 45s were withdrawn from service. However, No. 45106 was selected for reinstatement for railtours, and staff at Tinsley treated her to a celebrity paint-job, with her receiving a version of her original green livery. Unfortunately she sustained fire damage on 20 February 1989, and this time her withdrawal was final, bringing to an end the thirty-year career of the Peaks on BR. (Martin Corbett)

Tyne Yard, at Lamesley to the south of Gateshead, was one of the favourite haunts of my Dad and I when I was a young lad. The bridge carrying Smithy Lane across the marshalling yard, while providing a great view of the main line, gave only a frustratingly distant view of the shed there. This photographer was fortunate to be granted permission to visit in June 1970, and among the residents there were Class 03 D2104 and green Class 24 No. 5104. As Nos 03104 and No 24104 they were withdrawn in 1975 and 1976 respectively. (Mike Mather)

Having once been the home depot of the infamous Metropolitan-Vickers Co-Bo diesels, Carlisle's Upperby depot closed in 1968, being replaced by the new shed at Kingmoor. The location hosted an open day in September 1982, at which a variety of locomotives were present. One of the less glamorous exhibits was No. 20067, in the company of Class 86 electric No. 86204, appropriately named *City of Carlisle*. (David Tweddle)

When I beheld this scene for myself, it was in the gloomy twilight of a dank February day, so any attempt at photography was futile. This is Wath, near Barnsley, in May 1970. The photographer has captured Class 31, 37 and 47 diesels, along with Class 76 electrics in a variety of liveries – typical of that transitional period in the late 1960s and early '70s. Everything in this photograph has since been obliterated. (Mike Mather)

Willesden depot in north-west London served the electrified main line out of Euston, and was only a few hundred yards from the Western Region's Old Oak Common. Both featured in the March 1980 itinerary followed by my mates and I. Seen *c.* 1977, electric locomotives of Classes 86 and 81 share the clean interior with No. 25177. (Rex Holt)

Also in Willesden shed, celebrity Class 86 No. 86235 *Novelty* shows off her gaudy livery in December 1982. She received this treatment and the name as part of the 1980 celebrations marking the 150th anniversary of the Liverpool & Manchester Railway. The original *Novelty* was Braithwaite & Ericsson's unsuccessful entrant, and rival to Stephenson's *Rocket*, in the Rainhill Trials. (David Tweddle)

Right: Sporting a large patch of green undercoat, No. 25180 is seen inside her birthplace, BREL's Derby Works during an open day on 4 September 1982. In retrospect this would prove to be a waste of paint, for she was withdrawn two months later after a mere seventeen years of service on BR, having been delivered in 1965 as D7530. (David Tweddle)

Below: That same September 1982 Derby open day featured No. 45103, presumably in the works for an overhaul. Nos 56083 and 25036 can be seen beyond, with APT-P set No. 370003 glimpsed in the left distance. The haphazard TOPS renumbering scheme applied to Class 45s meant that No. 45103's previous identity was D116. She was built at Crewe in 1961 and remained in service until 1988. (David Tweddle)

One of the more interesting sights at the 1982 Derby open day was the pair of former Class 252 prototype High Speed Train power cars, by now withdrawn from departmental use as ADB975812 and ADB975813. They were built in 1972 at Crewe as Nos 41001 and 41002, later becoming Nos 43000 and 43001. In 1973 the pair broke the world speed record for diesel traction, attaining 143 mph at Northallerton. No. 41001 is preserved, representing the beginning of one of BR's more successful eras. (David Tweddle)

This shot taken inside BREL Doncaster in April 1983 gives some idea of the work involved in overhauling or refurbishing a diesel locomotive. This is No. 50050 *Fearless*, formerly D400, missing her bogies, buffers and probably minus her power unit too. Like most first-of-class locomotives, she lost her numerical identity under TOPS renumbering. She is one of many Class 50s in preservation. (David Tweddle)

27 February 1982 is a date etched on the memories of Deltic aficionados, for thousands congregated at Doncaster to pay their last respects to the fifteen members of the class not already reduced to scrap. Less than two months earlier, the 'Deltic Scotsman Farewell' railtour had brought down the curtain on the Class 55s' glorious career on BR. Little did we dream at that time that we would be able to enjoy six Deltics in preservation over thirty-six years later. This shot shows two of those survivors. Green No. 55002 next to No. 55016, with the less fortunate No. 55005 nearest the camera. (David Tweddle)

In contrast to the sad sight of locomotives being disposed of, BREL's works also gave the opportunity of seeing new locomotives under construction or just completed. I saw numerous Class 56s being built at Doncaster in 1978 and here we see brand-new No. 58001 there in April 1983. She was seen languishing in a siding in northern France in 2018. (David Tweddle)

BREL Eastleigh is the setting for No. 71001, formerly E5001, under overhaul on 13 August 1974. She was the second of the class, with E5000 being one of the ten Class 71s rebuilt as Paxman-engined Class 74 electro-diesels. The '71s' originally had pantographs for sidings with overhead catenary as well as collector shoes for the Southern Region's third rail. No. 71001 is now preserved in the National Collection. (Arnie Furniss)

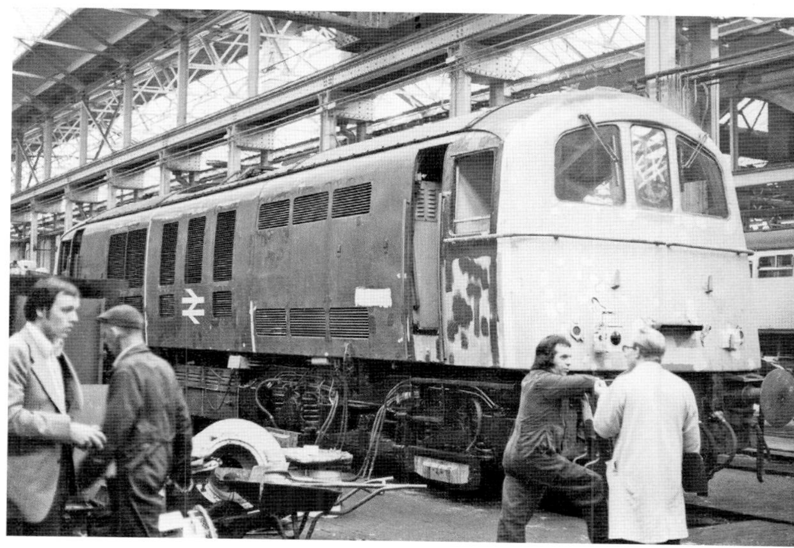

Newly overhauled and repainted, No. 73002 stands proudly outside Eastleigh Works on 16 November 1985. Of the six members of the original 73/0 subclass, five are preserved, including No. 73002, which resides at the Dean Forest Railway. They shared the same 600 hp English Electric diesel engine as the SR's diesel-electric multiple units. (Lewis Bevan)

No. 33023 is at Eastleigh for attention on 9 August 1977, alongside one of the aforementioned SR DEMUs. No. 1001 was one of the six-car Hastings line units, built to a narrower profile for the restricted loading gauge on that route. The three plain windows between the open doors on the power car allowed natural light into her engine compartment. 1001 is preserved and main-line certified. No. 33023, meanwhile, was scrapped in 2005 after forty-four years in service. (Rex Holt)

Anyone visiting BREL Glasgow in July 1972 would have been treated to the sight of this long line of doomed North British Locomotive Co. Class 29s, headed by No. 6103. Twenty of this class of fifty-eight had been re-engined with Paxman power units to extend their unspectacular lives by a few years. No NBL-built BR main line diesels lasted long enough to be preserved. (Laurie Mulrine)

I always loved to visit Glasgow Works, also known as St Rollox, and the open day there on 27 June 1981 was very memorable. No. 27009, formerly D5355, looks forlorn as she awaits the inevitable oxyacetylene torch, which came six months later. She had been withdrawn from service in July 1980, having spent her nineteen-year career at Eastfield. (Colin Alexander)